SUCCEED ON PURPOSE

SUCCEED ON PURPOSE

WHY ARE YOU A SUCCESS?

CHRISTINA MARIE

EDITED BY CHARLES E. SMITH, II

Printed in United States of America
 by 48HrBooks (www.48HrBooks.com)

ISBN (978-0-692-74864-0)

DEDICATION

This book is dedicated to my husband, Alvin Norman. His patience allowed me to complete this book with ease. This book is also dedicated to our three children who have adjusted their lives along with mine to see this project completed.

TABLE OF CONTENTS

ACKNOWLEDGEMENTS

I'd like to say thank you to:

The Lord Jesus who has given me every gift that I possess;

Each person who answered the question "Why are you a success?";

My friends and family who support my writings and events;

All of you who continue to purchase materials and support the *Live ON Purpose* Movement!

INTRODUCTION

Why are you a success?

Take a moment and think about that question. It's amazing how after speaking to dozens of people and asking them that same question, there were no two answers the same. In fact, many people told me it was quite difficult to answer. One woman I spoke to told me she could not think back over her life of over 50 years to deem herself successful. After giving her some encouragement and reminding her there were many successes in her life, she was able to provide me a very powerful response. The biggest issues was getting people past how they see themselves and on to how God sees them. He sees all of us (flaws and all) as a success because He does not make mess!

I love it! We need more thought provoking questions thrown our way to put us back on track to the BIG life we are destined to live.

What I've learned is success is not a compilation of all your good works or a summation of all the things you did right in life, but it really is just a decision to be better today than you were yesterday. It is a mindset that is working whether you feel successful or not. Your entire being lives out success because that's what you were created to be.

No one mentioned becoming famous as a sign of success. This is because there is so much more to it than that. Don't allow the media, especially social media, to fool you in to thinking the only way to measure success is to determine what materials you have.
Material items can be taken, damaged, or become worthless. Your self-worth is priceless.

There were many times while writing this work that I felt less than successful, but who said success is based on feelings. I'm so glad it's not. Our feelings change like the wind and we as people can be so unpredictable at times.

We find ourselves in traffic before work and immediately "feel" it's going to be the worst day ever. By lunch, our spouse surprises us with our favorite meal, and we are on cloud 9. We are very emotional and change so often we can't keep track. This is why success has less to do with how we feel and more to do with how we think. As you read this book, make mental notes of changes you can make right now. Don't let another New Year's resolution list come across your lap without first diving into this book and making much needed changes to the way you think.

I thought about how I should answer the question myself and I came up with this list.

Why are you a success? I am a success because...

- I am a child of Jesus Christ, and He has given me numerous reasons to be a success. He has forgiven me for all of my mess.

- I am not afraid to tell myself I am a success. Even in my lowest moments, I recall times in life I had success. This is important for those times you feel less than your best.

- I accomplished goals despite how much fear I was in while doing it.

- I use my gifts and talents to help others Live ON Purpose. Gifts are made to be given. What good is a gift if you keep it to yourself?

- I constantly show love and consideration to others and find ways to remind them they are great!

You see, what's most important is to know you are a success even when you fail!

Begin by:

1.   Defining Success

2.   Being Disciplined enough to succeed

3.   Being Organized

4.   Being Intentional

5.   Losing the Excuses

6.   Making Waves

7.   Carrying less baggage

8.   Knowing who you are

9.   Determining the relationship between success and money

10. Identifying what's stopping you

FORWARD

By Charles E. Smith, II

What makes me a success?

For me, it is a straight forward question with a straightforward answer. I am successful because I made the decision to submit to God's plan for my life, and as He has promised in Psalm 37:4, He has truly given me the desires of my heart.

Don't get me wrong: Like everyone, I had my own plans for what I thought I wanted to do with my life, and to be honest, those plans were not that bad. I figured out the things that I needed to do, the best way to do them, and the timeline I needed to do them in. And on top of all that, I was going to ask God to bless my plans.

But even with my plans being good, my methods being solid, and my timeline being realistic, there was the sense that I was wrong. There was the feeling that I was missing something, and if I didn't find out what it was, the rest of my life, even with all my good plans, would be ruined.

Even though I didn't understand it at first, I slowly began to realize that in all my planning, strategizing, and wanting God to bless what I was doing, I had forgotten the most important thing: Asking God what His plan for my life was.

I had heard the scripture several times. Jeremiah 29:11: For I know the thoughts that I think toward you, saith the Lord, thoughts of peace, and not of evil, to give you an expected end. So I realized that

God had a plan my life. Do you hear me? God had a plan for *my* life. A plan that was all good, and plan that He himself had made for me. The question was, did I trust Him to bring it to pass?

So I took a chance. I forgot about all the things that I wanted to do, and submitted to God's plan for my life. It was rough and tough at first, but only because God was preparing me for what He had for me. In time, the blessings started rolling in, and I began to see the desires of my heart in every area of my life.

Seventeen years later, I am continuing to see the desires of my heart in the majority of the areas of my life, with the knowledge that I will see the desires of my heart in every area of my life. It is because of God's plan for my life and His faithfulness after I submitted to Him that I am successful in my life.

God has a specific plan for your life and wants you to be successful. Do you have the faith to submit to Him and see that plan come to pass?

Charles Smith is the Senior Manufacturing Engineering for a world leading manufacturing company, an officer in the U.S. Air Force Reserves, the President and CEO of Christian Love Books, LLC, and Author of He That Findeth A Wife: A Christian Guide To Finding The Helpmate God Has For You. *A graduate of Tuskegee University and Southeastern Oklahoma State University, he is married to his college sweetheart Layana, and they are the parents of two beautiful children.*

1

WHAT IS SUCCESS?

Why are you Successful?

1. *Using my gifts to help others and to better my quality of life.*
2. *Never regretting any experience, but utilizing it as fuel to do better and to be better.*
3. *Forgiveness of yourself and others.*
4. *Never giving up on your vision and purpose.*

Courtney B.
Implementation Consultant for a Technology Company

What I really should be asking is "How do *YOU* define success?" You see, success is a personal and individual endeavor that starts on the inside of a person and becomes evident outwardly. Webster's Dictionary defines success as "a favorable or desired outcome; the attainment of wealth, favor, or eminence". Simply put…it is reaching your goals and having some cash to go with it! This could involve a large goal such as going to or finishing college, landing your dream job, getting married and starting a family, or something as simple as getting to work on time consistently. The accomplishment of either could be considered a successful event to different individuals.

This means you must to have goals to be attained!

Success is the ability to push past uncanny circumstances in order to reach a destination of value and worth. You cannot possibly believe success can be attained without challenges. You are going to go through things, have rollercoasters of ups and downs, and make major mistakes. These are what will make you such a great success. Our experiences begin to shape and mold who we are and what we think. Your thoughts are where it all starts. If you change your mind and thoughts, you change your life. You will never be able to call yourself a success if you are always staying in one place. You must be flexible and willing to move as your environment moves and changes. Don't get me wrong, I am not saying the way to success is to follow the crowd. I am saying that you must be willing to remain relevant. You must study your craft enough to know when you must adjust. It is key that you find yourself in places that will lead to success instead of being stuck on the roadside of failure. Success is a road to be traveled.

I remember when I made the decision to transition from my secure positon as an educator in a private school to stay home with my newborn for a year. This was one of the most frightening decisions I've ever made. It was most difficult not only because my financial state was about to change significantly, but additionally because I had tried this before. I constantly thought about how I was going to make it work this time. The one thing our mistakes and challenges teach us is what NOT to do the next time. I had turned in my final notice two other times within 10 years. The first time I simply was tired of what I had been doing. I knew I loved to teach but was not interested in writing lesson plans, attending football games, and having report card conferences until 8pm. I felt I was standing still; not really moving toward success as I had described it in my mind. I often asked myself, "What am I supposed to be doing?" I knew it was something a bit different, but had not put my finger on it just yet. It's amazing how we really do know what's best for us, yet we allow fear and other negative feelings to get in the way. Even though I knew there was more I was to do, I asked to retract my resignation (the first time!). My reality of financial needs kicked in really quickly. The second time I resigned, I turned in my notice (again!) and was determined I would leave this time.

About 4 years had gone by and I told myself I was going to make this happen. And I did, or so I thought! I spent two months (the summer months) MAKING myself find another job. Well, I now know that was one of my mistakes. I thought success was going to be found in a new job. This had to be the answer to all of my struggles, right? There was so much to learn at this point in my life about how to really succeed and how much I had already succeeded without even realizing it. I wish I had this book to read back then because I would have make choices differently. I went on to stress myself out looking for work. When I ultimately found nothing, I begged for my position back (again!). I felt stuck. I felt there was no real success in sight. How could I leave a job twice only to come right back? Want to know what makes it more interesting? I left once more. This time for a much better reason. I had our last child. I was so glad when I found out she was due during Easter break. Oh what a relief to be able to spend time home for the rest of the school year. I could finally take a break without regret. I then made a decision that I would not return to work the following year. I just wasn't happy. (*Note*: Up until this point, I never took in consideration that my inability to find happiness had NOTHING to do with my job!) Please know it had less to do with the job and more to do with ME. During that time home with the new baby, God began to show me the Live ON Purpose brand. I was terribly excited about the change he was showing me in my life. So when I walked away this time, it was a done deal, or so I thought.

All too often we allow the deceptive thoughts of fear to take over and rule our decisions. I am sure you can guess what I did next. I took a year off but went back to the job once again. Why?? Why would I continue to run back to a space in life where I felt unfulfilled? The answer lies in my perception of happiness and success at that time. It lied in the reminder that I absolutely adored the children I worked with and the CEOs I worked for. I thought success was defined by making a lot of money. That's it! We will talk later about how misguided this mindset was. What I was missing was not something the job/career could ever give me. This is why the cycle of leaving and returning continued to happen. Thank God for the amazing employer because they saw potential in me and accepted my back each time. But, I could not see past the smoke. I needed self-acceptance. I needed total freedom to be exactly who I wanted to be. It wasn't that the job was stifling me. I WAS STIFLING ME! It was my own fault because of the way I thought about myself and other things. Let's wrap this up by saying I left the job a fourth time. I had to be okay with stepping out of a place of comfort and financial stability into a world of the unknown. God had already dropped in my spirit what my next step would involve but because it was unfamiliar to me, I was scared to trust the process.

There is purpose in the process.

Nobel Peace Prize winner Albert Schweitzer says, "Success is not the key to happiness. Happiness is the key to success. If you love what you are doing, you will be successful." Many people focus on the money! But if money always equals success, why do some wealthy people take their own lives? Why are many of them depressed and estranged from their families? Are you still considered successful if you are rich and unhappy? I do believe wealth is a benefit and result of success. It will find you. In fact, it is in search of you know if you are in the right place when it is in motion. But the success has to be about more than just earning more cash. There should be peace and contentment.

What Is Success?

Are you still successful if you finished college but never wanted to go in the first place? What if you make 6 figures but hate waking up to go to work? My point is, DEFINE YOUR OWN success. There should be a non-negotiable that you will LOVE what you do. I'm not telling you to quit your job or to leave the situation you're in, but I am telling you to put your own happiness at the top of the "to-do" list for your life. Don't worry about what everyone else is telling you to do. Take their advice with a grain of salt and consider the source. They are simply trying to help, but remember the picture is painted differently for everyone. Don't try to mold your success just like another person's. You will become frustrated because theirs is not for you! The struggles that allowed them to reach their level of success are not yours either. Never forget that people love to tell their story in a bright light. Very few share what happened in the dark. You will hardly learn about what it took for them to reach the height they've attained. I don't want you to only view success as a finality, but also as a road to be traveled. Get on it, and move. You will see people and places you did not imagine. It is hard for you to imagine big when you keep yourself cramped in a small space where you do things you don't love, only focus on money, and have little happiness.

Sometimes I sit back and watch other people while thinking to myself, "I want to be like that or I wish I was that way." I look at their behaviors and actions wishing I were just as organized or pristine as they are or maybe wishing I was just as carefree and relaxed. The problem with this behavior is someone else is watching me thinking the same thing. This is why it's so vital to just "do you". When I make the mistake of comparing myself to others and wishing to be or have what belongs to them, I lose sight of what my purpose is. My purpose is like none other because there is no other me! So, I begin to shake it off and re- frame my mind. I become grateful for my goofy side as well as my overly serious side at times! I begin to be okay with my "OCD-like" tendencies because they all define ME. Confidently define yourself! Don't let others do it for you and avoid doing it based on anyone else in the process.

5 Signs of a successful person:

1.   *They get up and go because of a strong internal drive*

2.   *They set attainable, written goals*

3.   *They communicate effectively*

4.   *They do not make excuses*

5.   *They define THEIR OWN success*

Can you find yourself on this list?

2

ARE YOU DISCIPLINED ENOUGH TO SUCCEED?

Why are you Successful?

What makes me successful...? The word that describes what makes me successful is Family. Taking care and providing for my family is what motivates me to work so hard and grind the way that I do. Knowing that I have them to look out for as well as looking up to truly motivates me to be successful and do the best in everything that I do. My drive, my ambition, my work ethic, my faith, my heart and the love for my family are all the tools I use to be successful.

Quincy J.
Chef

Are You Disciplined Enough To Succeed?

Discipline is no more than a change in mindset and a way of living!

Why do you think you find yourself starting and stopping things often? Have you been on a fitness plan, did well for a while, and then just stopped? What about planning for the future? You wrote it all down and began to move forward, then all of you efforts just ceased. You picked up a book but never finished it. It could have been for valid reasons, but in many cases it was because you lacked discipline. There is no magic to it. It is a personal battle you must fight and WIN in order to be successful.

The dictionary defines discipline as "the practice of training people to obey rules or a code of behavior..." So that brings me to the next point; What rules or code of behavior do you determine for yourself? What standards do you hold for yourself? What are you training yourself to do and be? Discipline is equivalent to muscle memory. You do it automatically once you have trained yourself to do so. You must negotiate with yourself about those things you will ALWAYS do and things you just WON'T do! Discipline will not allow you to do things such as drink to intoxication, grab your keys and drive yourself home. Discipline will not allow you to miss a deadline or be late for a meeting without a sound cause. Discipline will keep you from rushing in the morning or losing your keys. As you can see, discipline and organization walk hand in hand. I love to have a place for everything. Those of you with children in the home know this is a nearly impossible feat to keep consistent, but even small children can learn discipline and organization. In fact, this is when it starts. It becomes habitual and irritating when there is a lack of it.

So, if you did not pick up on this while growing up, it may be more difficult to make the change, but it is very doable. Start with your daily activities. Find out what you do nearly every day, and make a routine out of it. Be disciplined about your time spent practicing on the golf course or even about having date night with your spouse. It is vital. There is no way you will reap the full benefits of true success if you navigate life without a disciplined mind and organized life.

You must first convince yourself you can do this! You WILL be disciplined and you WILL succeed! Figure out what is the bottleneck and get rid of it. If it is laziness, selfishness, pride, relationships, whatever it is that is keeping you from being disciplined, get rid of it. It will also keep you from being successful. Most often it is YOU that keeps yourself from being successful. You are getting in your own way. You just don't push yourself hard enough to do what you know is best. In my first book, *Live ON Purpose*, I discuss the importance of a mentor. If discipline and organization are a huge issue for you, find someone who does it well, and ask for help. You are not supposed to know it all, but it is important that you determine who may have the ability to direct or assist you. I tell people all the time about how much I love to organize. In fact, at one point in life, I was looking to be a certified organizer. I was going go into people's homes and organize their mess which in turn organized their life. I will have to say I quickly walked away from doing this professionally because of the liability and need to constantly be in a stranger's home. I was a bit uncomfortable. But, a few of my close friends have benefited from this love of mine!

Your purpose is designed to MAKE you a success. In my book, *Live ON Purpose*, you will find 8 key steps to identifying your purpose, but if you are not disciplined enough to read it and use the tools given, it will not work for you. Not only will you not identify your life's purpose, but you will keep someone else back from theirs when you are out of place. We are interdependent people and need each other tremendously. Don't be selfish in thinking your lack of task completion only affects you. IT DOESN'T! It affects everyone who comes in contact with you or is supposed to come in contact with you as well!

Constantly remind yourself why you do what you are doing. Each day won't be simple, but remember your "WHY" so you can be disciplined enough to succeed! What is the point of constantly striving for success if you don't know why you are doing it? Let's use an analogy. When I was in school I loved Math but was not the best at it. I remember a time in 7th grade, I finally received an "A" on my report card. I was too thrilled about my accomplishments.

Are You Disciplined Enough To Succeed?

That thrill ride came to an abrupt end on the playground when my teacher said that he understood I received an "A" but not to get used to it. What did he really mean, I wonder? Did he push me over the mark and give me that half point or was he going to make it his mission to make Math so hard I could never receive another "A" again. Ever! I believe he chose the latter because I never did have another "A" in Math. Over the years, I sat in many Math classes and had the same reoccurring thought... "Why do I need to know this?" Who cares what percent of 32 gives me 8. The square root of a number doesn't put money in my bank account." I just could not understand why I was doing it and how it could help. Until...

When real life hit, it became clear!

I would need this information to be sure I knew how much my discounted shirt should be once I arrived at the cash register so I was not cheated out of my change. Okay, I needed to understand square roots in order to be accepted into college without prerequisite courses. I got it! I didn't like that it took so long, but I'm glad the "why" became clear.

The same will happen for you. Your "why" will become clear. Once it does, keep it at the forefront of your mind. Let it drive all of your decisions, your relationships, and your purpose. Not having a why or not allowing it to drive you is the same as a person with a map who has nowhere to go. You are lost even though the tools are in your hand. Haven't you spent enough time lost and moving yet going nowhere? Your honest answer is probably yes. That's why this book is so important. I don't want you to keep moving on the elliptical machine of life, moving your legs and arms, falsifying forward motion. If you choose not to determine your why now, you will be in this same place next year. A year may seem far off, but just check your age a moment. How many years did you come up with? Didn't it go by quickly?

Get yourself disciplined enough to succeed. Once you know why you are striving for success, you can put a plan in place to get you there. You can line yourself up for a prosperous future.

Without discipline, you lack the foresight needed to get things done. You will allow every distraction to pull you away from not only your *why*, but your eventual destiny. It is quite natural for most people to come up with grand ideas yet never go after them. Think back on how many great ideas you've had over the years but did not chase after them. Why didn't you? Part of the reason is probably when you counted up the cost of what it would take from you to complete the idea start to finish, it was no longer worth your time and energy. Once we realize something is going to require a lot out of us, we tend to back out. We lack discipline. You are not by yourself. Discipline is a learned behavior. It is like a muscle that must be exercised often to become strong. Exercise discipline in your day to day life. Begin simply with times you wake up and go to sleep. Make yourself disciplined in studying your craft or business. You see, discipline and organization go hand and hand.

3

GET ORGANIZED

> *Why are you Successful?*
>
> *Referring to being a fitness instructor I would say I'm successful because I strive the make everyone feel welcome, always encouraging participants to get out of their comfort zone to reach their fitness goals. Above all I teach for the love of helping people stay healthy and active.*
>
> **Jackie Z.**
> *Fitness Instructor*

For many people, the thought of living a life of organization and structure is frightening. It makes some feel their creativity will be stifled. But this is the farthest from the truth. In fact, being organized will give you the freedom to express your creativity even more. Using a few simple steps to get you started, you will be "finding" more time in the day to do what you want and having a freer mind to do it. So…

1.   **Take a deep breath…**You have to relax. Contrary to what most believe, being organized is not about being uptight and having a very angled view on life. It is about taking charge of every moment and giving it no more power than you are willing to allow. John C. Maxwell says, "If you don't decide how your day will be spent, someone else will." Take a moment to make a solid decision. This is going to be the catalyst that moves you through the other steps. You must be in a peaceful state when you are thinking about getting things organized. Let's not talk about organizing your LIFE yet. Just start with your desk at work. Then move on to a closet, a room, garage, etc. Start small and tackle larger things as you become more comfortable. It's okay if you don't get it right the first time. Again, take a deep breath and try it once more. Studies have said it takes at least 21 days of doing something for it to become a habit. Living an organized life will become habitual if you let it. Stay calm. There will be days you find no inkling of organization and stability at all. It's called LIFE! It happens to the best of us. Just don't give up.

Know that those around you may have a different view of what organized is. My husband loves an "organized mess". Only he can find things in his space, but it works as long as I don't have to go be a part of that space. If he sends me to his closet, I find absolutely nothing. In fact, I become flustered and frustrated just looking at it. Then I remember to take a deep breath, relax, and move myself from the space. I decided I would be organized only in MY endeavors, not HIS! It works, and it keeps me from controlling someone else's "organized mess." You may find you will need to do the same to keep peace at home, at work, or even with your children.

---

2. **Write it down...**What good is completing High School, college, or beyond if there is no WRITTEN RECORD of it. Is it still valid? No, documenting and writing important items down makes it real and valid. Once you have made the decision to get more organized, write your goals down (or type them if you choose!). Write your goals for getting organized down, but write your *daily* goals down as well. After you complete your morning ritual, make time to write out your top 7 goals for the day. I call it SIT (Seven Important Things). Who are you willing to give your attention to today? If you haven't written it down as a top priority, maybe that phone call or that lunch date needs to wait. Check off items as you complete them. Watch how this gives you the sense of accomplishment you have been looking for.

This has to be done *every day*. As a life coach, one of the first ways I introduce organization to my clients is purchasing them a planner. One woman said, "Whatever you do, don't make me use a planner!" Of course my answer was that she would still receive the planner, but I ensured her I would help her learn to use it. We already live very busy lives and the thought of adding one more thing to it daily is scary for some people. That is completely understandable. The problem is without tools such as this, we will continue to allow ourselves to make excuses as to why tasks did not get done, goals reached, or why we are chronically late to events. See, many people want to change until they find out what it takes. Don't let this be you. You can take time to write important tasks and reminders down daily. I promise you it will ease your mind and allow you to take those deep peaceful breaths we just talked about. You can do it. Do it every day.

3. **Start each day over and forgive yourself...**Yesterday's inadequacies cannot be the only driving force for your new day. If it is, you will feel that your day is already starting off behind. Instead, think of it as a new day with new goals. You can't change yesterday and don't know what tomorrow brings. You can only account for today; therefore, it is okay if your daily goals begin to look uniformed as you may have some of the same important tasks daily. If you find that you constantly have incomplete work from the day before, you need to evaluate if you are really working on what's most important. You may be allowing yourself to be distracted with conversations, lunches, work, etc. that is keeping you from accomplishing what you have written to be important to you.

You will not get it right each day. It's okay. There will even be days you quit the idea of being organized and fall back to your old habits, and that's okay too. But if you really know progressing forward is for you, you will pick yourself up and get back on track. It is no different from completing the hardest Math or English class in your life. There comes a point when you get tired of it all. You have to remember anything great is worth working hard for. You have created a habit for the last however many years, and it will take time to change it. Forgive yourself when you fall and encourage yourself along the way. Keep people around you who will not badger you and will not put you down. In a later chapter, we will discuss how vital it is to keep the right people close to you.

If discipline is the muscle in your left leg, organization is the one in the right. You must exercise them concurrently in order for them to work at their best. I can always spot a person who is disorganized. Beyond surface level of messy desks, messy car, etc. they express their thoughts in a disorganized manner as well. When asked a question, a disorganized person tends to "fish" for the answer. They talk in circles often times repeating the same information yet giving no clear facts at all. These people will tend to do tasks over again instead of looking for a previous version to simply revise. Although it would be easier to simply update a former copy, they have no idea where to find the original. You see, it's not hard to spot someone who is disorganized. Success involves being genuinely happy. One cannot find joy not knowing where to find what they need when they need it.

Organize your mind, Organize your life!

18

4

BE INTENTIONAL

Why are you Successful?

Living and meditation in the word when we do that then we make our way prosperous and have Good success, also having a balance along with diligence and hard work.

Yashama R.
Cosmetologist

What is the first response a fearful child gives after being asked why they did what they did? It is typically…"I don't know." Well, for you that answer is just not good enough. You are a person with purpose. Ask yourself why you did what you did. Why did you make the decision you made? Why are you in the career you are in? Why are you where you are? If you are unsure of the answer, spend time assessing your previous steps. How did you get where you are mentally, physically, spiritually, financially, or even educationally? You won't know how to move forward properly and precisely with purpose if you are unclear about what brought you to your now. Figure out why you are not *exactly* where you want to be. Is it fear, lack of preparation, or lack of desire? Maybe you've simply been misguided or misinformed. Dig deep, look back and retrace your steps so the next time someone asks you why you are in the position you are in, you can give a definitive answer. Living ON Purpose is about living intentionally. Success is intentional! It doesn't just happen. While there are times in life great things happen with little effort on our part, they are very few. These are not to be solely relied upon or looked towards for your life's achievements. It is going to take persistent work and being able to know with confidence why you are making the moves you are making in this game board of life. While life itself is not a game, you will need to maneuver through it with intent and strategy in order to win!

The word intentional simply means "with reason and specific efforts." Do you have a specific reason for why you do what you do, or are you spontaneous and sporadic in your thinking and reasoning? It is important that you have a clear, concise reason for everything you are involved in. Without your reason, your "why", you are simply existing, moving through life haphazardly. The problem with this is you will constantly be moving yet not getting anywhere. You will be spinning your wheels while in park! It is vital not only to *have* a "why" but to *know* it. How would you answer if someone asked, "Why do you do what you do?" Do you find yourself going in circles to give an answer? If so, spend time right now establishing your reason. Really dig deep and ask yourself "Why?" Be honest.

It is not about anyone else other than YOU right now. You may end up finding out you've been working only to appease others. You may find you do it out of convenience. You don't know until you ask...yourself!

Once you've done the work of discovering your why, know that you will need to re-evaluate it from time to time. As life moves and changes, your "why" may change as well. For example, when I began teaching in 2003, I took a position as an elementary teacher when my background was in Technology Education. Why? Because, I had recently graduated college and gotten married. I knew I needed to be able to contribute to the marriage financially. I did not have a job prior to this opportunity and my husband was also looking for full-time work. My "why" was: I need income and I love children. Fast forward to 2008, I was still teaching but my "why" was slightly adjusted. At this time, we were financially above water and entering our 4th year of marriage with now two children in daycare! Yes, I needed income still but there was discounted daycare and the convenience of my children being on the same campus with me all day. My "why" became the need of fulfillment and experience in my career. My "why" was amended and that is okay. It is your duty and responsibility to always know your why and to initiate changes as you see fit. Without it, you will be lost. You will never experience the ability to Live ON Purpose if you simply just exist.

Being intentional means you are willing to plan. You are organized in such a way that your moves are deliberate and concise. Success is a planned accomplishment. Even the smallest successes require work and forethought. Running a successful business, moving up the corporate ladder, having a peaceful home, attaining a degree, being a good citizen...they all require an intentional effort. What are you thinking about regularly? Do your problems, issues, and favorite shows consume most of your thoughts? If so, there is no room in your mind for your success. Your thoughts are where your success begins. You must constantly plan to succeed.

5

EXCUSES, EXCUSES!

Why are you Successful?

For me success is fulfilling my dreams and goals not those places upon me by others. To some success may be a six figure or more salary with a family and house. Realizing this may take time for some where others see what they want out of life earlier. #myjourneyisnotyours

Anonymous Contributor

Yes, that's right. I just called you out on your number one problem for not getting those most important tasks done and dreams reached. It's your excuses. My pastor calls them high-class LIES! I like to think of them as the "scape goats" that go against your need to stay on task and get things done. Why do we let the clothes pile up when clearly they are clean and need to be folded? Why didn't we go back to school when we had fewer responsibilities in life? Why didn't we start the business when we knew the idea was fantastic? I believe it is because of excuses. We allow ourselves a way of escape by giving our psyche' so much information about why a thing canNOT be done that our body and world around us begin to agree as well. Why not use the same energy it takes to tell yourself why you canNOT do something and tell yourself why you MUST? The very things we talk ourselves out of most times are major parts of our life's purpose. I believe we are fully aware of this, but fear sets in. Fear is a negative idea that will come to mind, but is up to us to allow it to move in and stay. When you begin to hear yourself say phrases such as: "This is just too much", "I'm tired", or "I can't", it may *not* be the complete truth of the matter. Check your heart and be sure you are not allowing yourself to just make one more excuse. Excuses are like lies. Once you tell one, you must continue to tell them in order to keep your story straight. Don't allow this purpose-mutilation to occur in your life. Instead, fight back. Fight the thoughts of excuse and allowance. Hold yourself accountable.

Have you ever been invited to an event? You had intentions to attend, but simply forgot. When you see the person who invited you and they ask you what happened, what do you say? Do you tell a partial truth (which is also a partial lie) or are you completely honest in saying you didn't write it down and solely relied on your mental capacity to remind you of the event therefore forgot? More than likely you chose the first response. We don't like to look as if we don't know what we are doing. We really don't like to make mistakes. But why? We know we are not perfect, right?

At times, the reason people give excuses is not because of themselves but because of the people they are responding to. The person on the other side of the excuse may have given the person a reason to feel they must present themselves in a perfect way as if they have it all together at all times. The problem with this is it's all a LIE. No matter the reason or logic for the excuse, the end result is the same. Do not be overly concerned with people. It's not completely reasonable to say you shouldn't care about what people say, but you should not hold their opinion of you at a higher esteem than you hold your opinion of yourself. If you do, you will find yourself making more excuses than you could have imagined. Soon after, you will find yourself still stuck in the same place.

Excuses prevent forward movement!

Excuses keep us stuck in a place we could otherwise move on from. Recall the story of Adam and Eve in the Bible. God told them they had everything they needed to survive, yet He had one request; "Do not touch the fruit of the tree of Knowledge of Good and Evil." Seems simple enough since they were otherwise living in the lap of luxury, right? They did not have to work. They had no children yet. They had no bills. Everything they needed was PAID FOR! Amazing, right? For them that wasn't enough. The ONE thing God asked them not to do, they did anyway because of a decision. Our life is based on our decisions, both right and wrong. Our future is shaped and centered on our past and present decisions and choices. They made a poor choice that would ultimately shape the entire world. Once Eve listened to the serpent who told her what God said wasn't true, she believed him. Sometimes we make excuses because we we've been listening to the wrong people. The people who truly care about us have been pushed aside by our arrogance and pride. Since we were left listening to the wrong people, we made mistakes. Those mistakes led us to believe we needed to create excuses for our actions. When God began to question Eve about her choice to eat of the forbidden fruit, she blamed the serpent who came to speak to her. I mentioned earlier how important it is to listen to the right people, remember? Then God asks Adam why he also took part in this forbidden fruit, he says, "The woman you gave me..." We tend to blame those closest to us. Those who have been through it all with us. It's a backwards, twisted idea, but many hurt those they love most. It's more convenient feeling as though those people have always been there and always will be. Notice neither one of them used words such as *I* or *me*. They never did fess up. They just got caught! In fact, during this ordeal they tried to hide from their Creator. Read Genesis chapter 1 for the whole story, and notice their forward movement was abruptly slowed down. They no longer had the free life to live. You deserve to have the life you WANT. Not the one that is left over as a result of all your excuses. It's already been given to you. Go possess it.

I do not like to be in the presence of people who always have excuses of why they can't or why they didn't! I need go-getters and forward thinkers around me. People who aren't afraid to make mistakes and fail at times. Failure is one of the best teachers. It's okay to fail. Just try not to fail while doing the same thing each time.

Normally failure is a pure negative, but if you are honest, it is the failures that make your purpose more perfect!

Unlike Adam and Eve, some people say their excuses to themselves, and they become evident as fear. You can always tell a person who is walking in fear and making excuses when it's time to put in some work. They never want to be first, and they want to play it safe in the background. Don't confuse a humble heart with fear. They are not the same. Someone with a humble heart is still willing to do the work. They may want to be in the shadows or in the background but they are willing to put in just as much effort as anyone else. They just do not need or want the outward credit. Someone walking in fear will continue to make excuses about why things just can't work out.

My point here is just to be careful. Sometimes we make excuses unconsciously. We say we are just being "realistic" or "upfront" but what's the real harm in trying? That is what being a success is about. Get up and try it. Make no excuses about it. If you want it, it's yours!

6

MAKE WAVES

Why are you Successful?

First of all, my Faith, Trust and Dependence on God in every situation I encounter. Secondly, allowing the love of God to flow out of me so I can be a blessing to others that I encounter.

Valisha F.
Human Resource Director

From a young age, I remember feeling very uneasy when involved in confrontation or had to explain myself. One place it was most evident was in the exchanges between me and my mother. While she was an amazing and intelligent woman, her ability to communicate effectively was often flawed. When we disagreed, I would sometimes wonder if it was worth it to really try and have my point heard by her or not. The conversation in my mind involved decisions between standing my ground by saying what I felt about a situation knowing it would cause me to be punished for it or staying quiet in order to keep the peace. More often than not, I chose to keep the peace because at least then, I knew the confrontation or situation was over. This technique of keeping quiet began to show up in other parts of my life. It showed up with bullies at school. I did not stand up to them, I continually took the shortest road to exiting the situation which was to simply give in and say as little to rattle them as I could. It happened at work with co-workers if they had a difference of opinion, and I was not willing to defend my case or reasoning about a decision. I would simply say what others wanted to hear and do what they asked me to do without rebuttal in order to eliminate the presence of any confrontational exchange. I have always been taught to go with the flow and "Don't make no waves" in order to stay out of trouble. This is a mantra I often lived by, but why? Why was I so afraid to ruffle anyone's feathers, even if it meant mine would end up in a bunch because of it? I didn't want to bother anyone or find myself on their "bad side". You see while most people thought I was only a loud outspoken kid who loved the lime light, I really was not the type that was looking to stand out for greatness. But inwardly, I didn't want to stand out for bad either. As I got older, I was okay blending in and rarely being seen. But as you know, being a chameleon does not warrant you being a success. I went many years trying to figure out why (in my mind) everyone was better than me. Why could she sing better than I could? Why did she dance better than I did? Why were they invited in clubs for smart people? What I had to realize was it was nothing they did, it was me. I had made a decision very early on that I would subject myself to second place and be content there. After all, first place meant I may have to say and do a few things others didn't like or want to hear. My whole goal was to please people. I felt that if I made someone upset or disappointed them, I would not be putting myself in a place for success because you must please people in order to be considered a success, right? Boy, was I wrong. Really, really wrong! It wasn't until I learned that it takes boldness to be a success that I began down the right track. You will never please everyone. Simply do what you do from the heart and you are already well on your way to success. Sitting back and accepting 2nd and 3rd place would no longer cut it. I found this to be enlightening yet confusing. So you mean to tell me the child who was always told she was too mean is now given permission to say what she means to say? But that's going to hurt someone possibly, and hurt people leave. The harsh reality is that there are people you need out of your life anyway in order for your purpose to make you a success. Don't allow fear to keep you from your ability to communicate effectively. If the other person or people decide to remove themselves from you because of it, it is all the better. At least now you know where they stand in your journey to success. It is definitely a learning experience, but it's one worth learning.

Your purpose will put you out front; not only for your gain but for the gain of the greater cause.

For the sake of comparison, what is an ocean without waves? It is merely a motionless body of water with the potential to be something greater. It will lack life and meaning and become nothing more than a dying pool. Did you know waves were created by wind? The wind then transfers some of its energy to the water through **friction**. Friction, simply put, is a force that resists or moves against a particular motion. *(Okay, that was the Science teacher in me...carry on!)* Therefore we are going to "rub" people the wrong way sometimes. Yet, waves often draw people to the ocean. They are a creative and useful site. So are we, when we are not afraid of opposition, friction, and some forms of conflict. It is important that you not only know WHAT you believe in but that you are willing to fight for it.

What you won't fight for, someone will steal!

Do not consider everyone else's feelings before your own. You must feel good about your decisions with total confidence because you WILL have to express your feelings, whether positive or negative, from time to time. You may even have to get your point across in somewhat of an aggressive matter at times. But know it all comes from a good place and that you are not TRYING to "make waves." It is that you are fighting for your *purpose*. Once you identify it, there is no turning back. You must reach it.

Believe me, for some of you this will take some getting used to. Others, you are already experts in this area. You say what you mean and mean what you say. I always admired people like that. But whichever category you are in right now, the same holds true. You must speak up and at times speak loud. Use wisdom. If you are unsure of how to confront an issue or a person tactfully, do your research or ask someone who is very good at it already where they find their strength.

It boils down to "Not caring more about what others think of you than what you think of yourself!"

I'm so glad I am learning this lesson. Notice I said "learning". I have to constantly remind myself it is okay to express my opinion and thoughts even if contrary to popular belief. I do not go around hurting others or causing conflict, but I am not going to be afraid either. I stopped letting others control me with their feelings, and I suggest you do the same!

Seeking the approval of others was one of my first mistakes. But how could I avoid it? I constantly sought the approval of my number one supporter. When mom is happy, the house is happy, right? Right! So my goal became her happiness which would equal my approval. It was a win-win until it wasn't. It became a game between me and myself to see if she could be MADE happy. Somehow I put all of that responsibility on myself. I gauged my success and goodness on her response and ultimately anyone's response.

Positive response = success. Negative response = failure. And when there was no response = unworthy. I willingly and purposefully put my life in the hands of others over and over again hoping there was someone I could make happy every day, all the time forever. I now know how unrealistic this is, but during this time I continued creating this roller coaster of emotions within my mind. I now continue to use the words *I* and *me* because I take responsibility for those choices. While I was influenced and reared a certain way, it was me who ultimately decided not to change the cycle. I continued to make decisions based on what others MIGHT think or how they MIGHT respond.

Why give others that much power in your life? We are interdependent, needing each other to survive, yet we still have our own mind to make our own decisions. This is why the book holds the title, *Succeed ON Purpose*. Do it on purpose with great intent, reasoning, and thought. You have a choice to make.

You can play with your life as a puppet on strings constantly putting on a costume and performing before the crowd you call, family, friends, and co-workers, or you can be the director and call the shots in your own success.

Make a decision and stick with it!

7

NO EXTRA BAGGAGE

Why are you Successful?

Achieving your goals!

Sabrina W.
Medical Biller

Applying myself to all of my courses in school.

Kayla B.
Undergraduate Student

Who you keep close could be keeping you from reaching your life's purpose!

Want to find out who is and who isn't...??   Take this quick test!

1. Take a moment and examine the top 5 people you communicate with. These could be a spouse, friends, family members, co-workers, neighbors, etc. Write each name down.

1. _____
2. _____
3. _____
4. _____
5. _____

Now write down each individual's 2 BEST qualities

Person 1. _____   _____
Person 2. _____   _____
Person 3. _____   _____
Person 4. _____   _____
Person 5. _____   _____

2. Next, write 4 ways each person contributes positively to or enhances your life. (You really should be able to name more than four if time permits)

Note: If you are already struggling to come up with answers, this person may not need to be in your top five! They may not be contributing to your life as much as you need – just a thought!

Person 1. _____ _____

_____ _____

Person 2. _____ _____

_____ _____

Person 3. _____ _____

_____ _____

Person 4. _____ _____

_____ _____

Person 5. _____ _____

_____ _____

3. Lastly, rate this person 1-5 (1 being best able and 5 being least able) in their ability to help you reach your goals in life.

Person 1. _____
Person 2. _____
Person 3. _____
Person 4. _____
Person 5. _____

Take time to *reflect* on the answers you've written.

Now, that was just a quick test to guide you in letting go of some extra baggage. There are some people we keep around for convenience. Others because of familiarity. But we should focus more on keeping those around who encourage us to move forward and be our very best. These are not always the people with the most money or ones who have all the right answers for you, but they are genuine, organic people who care about you wholeheartedly. Your relationship with them is not one sided and they are not costly.

When you board an airplane, there is only so much baggage weight that can be carried before the ride become detrimental for all those involved. If you are carrying more than the allotted amount, extra money must be spent as well, right? Such is the same when WE carry extra baggage. At times we "carry" people around with us. We carry their ideals, their attitudes, and thoughts. We even carry with us how they feel (negatively) about us. It is time we "Let it go!" for real. If you carry these people, these thoughts around with you any longer, it will be detrimental for all those involved. In my book, *Live ON Purpose*, I talk about the fact that your decisions affect everything and everyone around you. It is never isolated to JUST you! So keeping baggage that should be let go affects all others who are **connected** to you as well. You need to be FREE to be creative. You need to be FREE to be effective. You need to be FREE to Succeed ON Purpose! Begin to look closely at your relationships and the negative life events you have kept so close. Some of them may need to be left at the terminal while you go fly FREE!

8

WHO ARE YOU?

Why are you Successful?

When you have arrived and are able to reach back and help others meet their dreams and goals. When you are able to see the fruit of your labor. When you are happy and content with yourself.

Anonymous Contributor

That's a loaded question. People have often argued whether we are a product of our environment or if our environment is a product of who we are. I believe it is both! We are interdependent. We need our environment to learn and in some cases live. Concurrently, our environment needs us in order for work to be fulfilled. Since this is the case, how do you know who you really are? As Miguel Ruiz Jr. says in the book *The Four Attachments*, you are a combination of all the attachments you've had and still have in life. All of your beliefs and values are a summation of what you've been taught, what you believed, and what you trusted of what you've been taught. You are a collection of your experiences and thoughts about those experiences. This is why two people can visit the same place and have very different memories.

I remember being offered a trip to Europe over Spring Break in high school. I didn't ask my parents for the money to go so I just listened to friend's stories once they came back from what sounded like the best time ever in France. They mentioned how wonderful the flight, the food, and the overall experience of leaving the country were. Their memories helped shape who they were at that very moment, but their experience was totally different from those who were in France on Friday, November 13, 2015 when terrorist attacks hit. People were being killed right in front of family members. One girl recalled the account of how she played dead for over an hour. During that, time she watched other people being murdered while trying not to breathe or cry. That experience forever changed the lives of many. Same place but different view.

What we really want is to be able to be the "real me" in front of everybody.

The reality is we often become chameleons based on the situation. So how do we become more comfortable being our "real me?" I'm glad you asked…So, let's get down to the nitty gritty (as my mom would say)!

Succeed Seed #1: KNOW what YOU think.
People can and will take advantage of the fact that you don't know
what you REALLY believe or want. When you are wishy-washy
about decisions, that's a sure sign you don't truly believe in what you
think. For example, if you and your spouse don't mind having more
children after your children are already grown, what's the problem?
There will be some nay-sayers and those with opinions which have
NOTHING to do with you. Please remember opinions are like butts.
Everyone has one! Be confident in what it is you want. Don't go
back and forth, or at least don't do it openly. People can smell fear
and know when you are unsure, waiting for someone to agree. They
are most likely not going to agree, so you have to know what YOU
think first and foremost with no reservations. Know that you know
that you know you truly believe in the decision you are about to
make or already have made. Don't tell everyone what you are
thinking right away, because it's not completely thought through just
yet. Be sure to count up the cost of your decision so you can defend
your decision if necessary. No matter how much you believe, there
will be disapproval from people. That's just PEOPLE! Even when
the negativity comes from close friends or family, you have to
eliminate it from your surroundings! I am not advising you to disown
your family, but you may have to create a different communication
schedule. Negativity cannot thrive in a positive-minded space unless
you allow it, therefore you have to remove it from around you.

Succeed Seed #2: Take Care of You
It is not that you are trying to be insensitive or ugly, but Succeeding
On Purpose can be so involved that you have little time to look
around at others. Be engrossed in what you love and ways you plan
to progress in life! By taking care of YOU first, you can be a better
person for those around you and those you love! What quality of a
CEO are you if you are constantly sick or heavily medicated? Think
about it. When we do not take care of our body, it lets us know. We
find ourselves slowing down, not feeling well for prolonged periods
of time, or even in the hospital. Your family needs you. Your
community needs you. Your career endeavors need you, but most of
all...YOU need YOU. There is no copy for who you are. You
cannot be recreated, so be sure to treat yourself right and put yourself

first (at least sometimes!) Seriously! We say it so much it's almost a cliché, "Take Care!", but do we do it? There is no job in the world that will not replace you. There is no school PTA that will not find a stand-in. There is not even a board meeting that cannot be handled without your presence. But there is a "real me" waiting for you to arrive. The moment you allow your authentic self to show up, success will become evident and more attainable. Many people talk about how they have multiple "selves." There's the work "self", the home "self", the social "self" amongst many others masks that we put on and take off throughout our lives. The problem with this is these "selves" have to constantly be managed. If you bring too much of your home "self" to work, they may find out what kind of person you really are! Imagine yourself as a puzzle of 1000 pieces finally completed and the masterpiece sits on your coffee table. It has taken you days, even weeks of concentration and work to put it together and someone comes in removing a piece. How does this make you feel? I would imagine the success you felt after putting in the final piece would now be depleted, you may even become angry because it is only complete with all pieces intact. This is how you will eventually feel when you are not expressing your genuine "self" at all times. You will begin to be angered by the thought of "I just want to be me!" So, I encourage you to spend time putting all of the "puzzle pieces" of you together in a way you can be pleased with your own work and efforts, and guard your masterpiece not allowing anyone to pluck pieces which change the beautiful picture we call YOU!

Succeed Seed #3: Be amazing

When you are great at what you do, people will talk. They will give some positive feedback, but unfortunately more will be negative. The important thing is…they're talking about YOU. Proverbs 18:16 says, "A man's gift makes room for him, and brings him before great men." Don't worry so much about WHAT they're saying. As long as they're saying SOMETHING, you've captured their attention! How many times in the news have you heard something negative about a clothing company, a big business, or a pop star, but you went to Google and looked it up. We live in an information world. People are always on the look-out for news (or drama, however you want to name it!) So give them some. Be amazing. The word amazing is defined as "causing great surprise or sudden wonder." Surprise people with how well you do what you do. Make them wonder how you are so great at the service you provide and the integrity you provide it with.

Succeed Seed #4: Stop Over-thinking it
No, really!! STOP! You will say things you did not intend to say in ways you didn't intend to say them…get over it. It's not the first time, nor will it be the last. There will be times you are embarrassed and feeling shamed. Pick yourself up, apologize and move forward. You are NOT your mistakes. It is easier said than done but no one said it would be easy! It must be done! Be sure your heart and intentions were in the right place. If they weren't, take care of your business and get it fixed. Give yourself a time frame that you will spend reflecting on what happened. Once that time frame has passed, LET IT GO! Over-thinking used to put me in a bad place. I would make a mistake in front of someone or say something in a conversation that I really didn't mean, and it would haunt me. Yes, literally haunt me. In my sleep, it would run through my mind about what I did or said over and over again. There was no way to take it back, and I was too proud and embarrassed to try to fix it, yet I just wouldn't let it go. According to the mind-sets.com website, we have 50,000-70,000 thoughts a day. Many of them at the same time or subconsciously. It's also states, "Ninety-five percent of these thoughts are repeated daily and reflect the mindset or beliefs we hold that lead to those 50,000 thoughts. Your mindset in turn governs your actions, which lead to your results in life. In short, if you have a mindset that limits your potential, then you will likely accept limited results in your life."

Succeed Seed #5: Evaluate who is worth listening to
First, you do not share your dreams and aspirations with everyone. They don't deserve to know. Just let them see it. By nature, people are very skeptical and tend to be "helping" but often are just dropping seeds of discouragement and fear. That will cause you to rethink everything. That's why Succeed Seed #1 was so important.

Secondly, know who you are keeping around you and who you can trust with your thoughts. Treat your ideas like a baby. You wouldn't let just anyone hold your child and talk to him or her would you? Of course not! Then there are only a select few you let "hold" and "speak to" your concepts and ideas. Those SELECT FEW may be some of the only people worth listening to. All other opinions should only be taken with a grain of salt. Keep your circle small. I tell people all the time, I don't really have a circle of friends…I have a line!

Why do you think campaign ads end their commercials with "I am _(their name)_, and I approve this message."? It is because we are trained from a young age to believe that someone else's approval is all we need in order to make the best decisions. We are inundated with social and political figures who put their stamp of approval on an item in hopes of us running behind that which they approved. It is happening all around you right now. The soda (or water) you are drinking had a well-known figure in their commercial to promote sales. The pie you had over the holidays may have had a famous singer on the front. But, is that all we are? A sale? No, of course not. But, we do often validate ourselves and our lives based on someone else's approval.

Make a decision and stick with it!

Look in the mirror and tell YOURSELF…I am _(your name)_ and I approve this message!

You are more than what you see. In fact, most people have no idea who they *really* are. You are a direct image of your Creator. When an artist paints a picture, the picture in some way represents them. While the picture may not look exactly like the painter, there are elements that will help you identify its maker. There are features that are only attributed to that particular artist. Those features are tied to his or her creative mind only. Their brush strokes and designs allow you to identify the creator of the masterpiece with ease. Most people never realize they are a masterpiece created by the Master Creator.

Who Are You?

You are a great success already. Do you know who you are? You are more than just a flawed exterior laid upon a more flawed interior. You are more than your less than perfect decisions from both past and present. And, you are more than what others judge about you! Those people don't really know you. You are still striving to know and understand yourself fully without regrets.

The seed for success is already in you! It is a known fact that when a plant is to grow, it must first begin as a seed. The seed then is well taken care of, watered, nourished, and given much sun to someday become what it was designed to become. But, for most plants, this does not happen overnight. Some take days, months, even years to bear fruit. Have you ever seen an apple tree bear oranges? No. You know why? The tree can only produce from what the seed has inside. While the seed is physically small and seems incapable of ever being anything of substance, in it is everything it will become.

Be careful of what seeds you allow to fall on the soil of your life!

It WILL produce what's inside of it. Our lives will too produce from what seeds are inside. Take note of what is before your eyes at all times. What do you spend time watching? TV, social media, and the internet (in general) have many eye-catching, luring traps. Watch what you allow through the windows of your soul (mind). Keep positive images in front of you. Images of success, love, and empowerment. Yes, it is just that important. Someone close to you is receiving the seeds you are dropping as well. You will know because the people close to you will be just like you. You begin to talk the same, have similar mannerisms. You didn't think that was a coincidence did you? You deposit seeds in one another and those seeds will too grow. Be sure they are seeds of love and encouragement. That's what you are destined to be: a person of love and constant encouragement to yourself and others! Aside from your eyes, you must intentionally monitor the seeds that fall on your ears. Guard what you hear. TURN IT OFF! You control that. Stay out of unproductive conversations. You are not a trash receptacle are you? Since you are not, why do you allow people to dump their trash in and on you? Think about an unproductive conversation you were in this week. That is time you will *never* get back. You may have already seen the "fruit" of that conversation. It may have resulted in not getting things done that are pertinent. It could have even shown up in your changed negative attitude after the conversation. These are subtle ways we are thrown off course of our purpose. God has already planted the purpose seed in us before we were ever born. You have an innate purpose that no one else can make flourish as you can. BUT, whatever seeds you have allowed to fall on your life, will take over that purpose until you "pull up the weeds."

In Acts 3 of the Bible, you find a man who sits daily at the gate called Beautiful and begs. He is at a low place in his life. Not only does he have nothing physically, but he also has no one around him who will help him move past his current state. In fact, they have helped him become more and more comfortable with his debilitating situation. He begs daily for his needs to be met through the giving of strangers. What's worse is that there are people who enable him every day, taking him to the place where he will beg. I would imagine there is also another group who takes him back where he resides until morning. Wouldn't it have been better for these people who brought him to his begging station to encourage and empower him as they travel each morning instead? Just what if they told him, "You're better than this!"? What if they told him about his untapped potential? These weren't just "anybodies". They were people this man interacted with day after day! He trusted them.

All too often, the people who are closest to us are not helping us tap into our greatest potential. They are so familiar with our daily routines that they find it hard to see us for who we REALLY are! If those whom you keep closest to you cannot provide encouragement, and their lives do not uplift others, you may want to re-evaluate why you keep them so close. They should not be enablers silently watching you waste your talent.

One day, while the man was begging, two great men came walking by. They saw and heard the man. When the man asked them for money, their response shocked the man and everyone around. They told him they had no money but had a powerful suggestion. They had the kind of concern that should have been given by the people who the beggar chose to let carry him to the gate every day. They simply said, "In the name of Jesus, walk!" They took the man by the hand, helped him up and instantly, the man's feet and ankles became strong.

It doesn't take a whole lot! An army of 5,000 nor a 3-hour long dissertation were necessary. It only required just a few empowering words from people who cared more about who he was to become than who he was at his present state.

If you don't have anyone who can strengthen you instantly, you will need to start by encouraging yourself. Know that God is the best encourager you can find. He will strategically place the right people in your life. It's your job to nurture these relationships. Don't be fooled by "look-a-likes" brought to you by the enemy. These relationships are not meant for your good and take you off course. You'll know the right people by their "fruit." What does the relationship produce? Do they bring you **TO** your problem or **OUT** of your problem?? They should just tell you..."YOU ARE BETTER THAN THIS!"

9

SUCCESS AND MONEY

Why are you Successful?

What makes me a success is setting a goal to accomplish something and pressing forward until I achieve them regardless of any obstacles. Truly believing with my whole heart that I can achieve anything as I rely on God and not my own strength is the only way to overcome the obstacles.

Janique C.
Studied Project Management

This is the kicker right here…MONEY! Money has been said to cause divorce, lead people to murder, tear children from their parents, and has even caused most of the wars and disputes among countries. That is powerful. The reason it is so powerful is because it falls in the hands of powerful people. Money itself has no special abilities. It is fluid and always moving. You can attest to that when as soon as you have income, there are bills to be paid. It often seems as soon as you receive it, there is somewhere else for it to go. It does take money to make money, so your money always has a job and place to be. But, it is tremendously important that it falls in to the right hands.

Many have said money is the root of all evil. The truth is this scripture is misquoted. In fact it says, "For the *love* of money is a root of all kinds of evil" (1 Timothy 6:10). Notice the small four letter word *love*. It can surely be missed if not carefully read. Love is a strong feeling of compassion and care for towards a person or thing. This is the most important part of the quote. People will kill over love. They will do things they would have never imagined themselves doing for the sake of love. So let's be clear. Success and money can go hand in hand, but the love of money will cause it all to go awry! Think about the one thing or person you love the most. What would you do for that thing or person to stay safe? What would you do to be sure you are always close by? This is how some feel about their money.

As I mentioned at the beginning of the book, many people judge their success by their bank account status. The downside to doing this is you are subconsciously telling yourself if this money were to ever go away, you are no longer a success of any kind. Sounds extreme, I know, but I've read about how people would kill themselves if they could no longer have access to the type of money they were once accustomed to. Their hard work and success or their family inheritance means the world to them. It's vital to know you can be a success with or without the money. So let's put this in perspective then.

Is money controlling us or are we controlling our money?

As people of success, we need not be controlled by an entity that is so fluid and easy to change. Money has no heart or soul. How can we allow it to control us and determine our success?

There are three ways to keep control of your money and not solely gauge your success on it:

1. **Get some help!** No one is born with knowledge of how to manage their money. But, some are fortunate enough to be surrounded by people who do. They are taught at a very young age the value of money and how to use it in the best way possible. Topics such as saving and investing are discussed at young ages. Children are given books to read and hands-on experience in the family business. Those who may not have had a start such as this, it is important that when you know more, you do more. One thing I regretted after college is that I did not take one business class. I felt left behind, so I read business magazines and talked to others who know more than I did about it. I had to get some help. Even now, I still am asking a lot of questions in order to stay current in the area.

Pride is the only thing that will keep you from asking for help. No matter what your current level of success, there are people who have, know, and do more than you. Don't be fooled into thinking you don't need anyone's help. A financial advisor will be more than willing to assist you in making the most of your money. Ask for help on what to do with large sums of money you acquire. I know you'd like to think you know exactly what you would do with 2.8 billion dollars, but you need a professional to help you. There are some things you need to do before you go off and buy your parents a new home on their own island, you know!

If you are not where you believe you should be financially, find someone who can help. There are so many programs to help you build credit as well. However, beware of scams! Do your research! I remember when my husband and I went through our financial hardship. We were so young and did not even realize what was happening. My husband and I were just starting out. We had been married nearly 3 years with a two year old. The term "Adjustable Rate Mortgage" was foreign to us, so our ignorance finally caught up with us. My husband left his full time job to pursue purchasing investment homes. It was going really well. Then...The market...Need I say more? It all went downhill fast for us. We ended up filing for bankruptcy and foreclosing on our home. We really thought there was no air above water during that situation. But, consistency worked in our favor. We began to pay off debts and long story short...began to see ourselves out of financial ruin. It took about 3 years, but it happened. During this time, we researched programs to help us to prepare to purchase a home again. We even studied the language banks used. We really did our homework the next time around. I am grateful we have not been in that situation again since.

But, we really relied on the knowledge of others. Friends and family who had been through similar situations also offered help in the area of what to do and what NOT to do.

2. **Use a budget!** Get it out of your head and onto paper. I know you THINK you have it all under control and maybe you do for now. But, don't forget success can come quickly. With more success will naturally come more money. **Ask yourself:** How will I spend it? How will I acquire more? Who needs to be paid? How much do I really need? This is just the beginning. There are so many reasons you need a budget not only for your personal use, but for your small or large business.

Business budgets typically are created on an annual basis so they can carefully outline the expected needs. Using an annual budget for business limits the amount of time spent creating and managing capital resources. Large companies may have employed accountants or other professionals to create the business budget, small business owners are usually responsible to complete this function themselves

Your budget is your roadmap. Would you drive from one corner of the U.S. to the other without GPS or a map? No, you wouldn't. Even if you were familiar with the route, things happen. What if a road was closed and you had to re-route? You need a plan, you need the map which not only shows you where you are going, but it also keeps you on track. A quality budget will show you where detours have been made. Too many of those and you won't get to your destination. The budget helps with timeframes. Allowing you to see how long it took to get where you wanted to be. They are living documents and can be adjusted to reflect real-time concerns.

With all this said, there is no reason you wouldn't have a budget for your household or business. Be sure to ask for help when needed and have your budget written (or typed of course) where it can be read and understood by all parties involved. Think about the people you lead whether it be your children or your employees, you have a responsibility to show them where you are leading them. A budget is the best way to show them where they are headed financially.

3. **Know your worth!** You are worth more than just your money. People sometimes forget they are more than just the sum of money in the bank. Lack of money can lead to such negativities as depression and suicide. But why? We are not aware of our true worth. Once you know your true worth, no one or no-thing will make you feel worthless; not even your money or lack of it. You are an amazing man or woman who has purpose in life. There is no price that would be enough to pay to replace YOU. Know there is only one like you therefore the world needs everything you have to offer. The world needs, your love, care, passion, and purpose to be spread everywhere you go. Because we are interdependent people, we need each other. Even just one piece missing and the puzzle is never complete. You are worth more than anything money can buy. No car, house, social status, or lack thereof should determine your worth. Don't determine your true worth with what others say about you either.

People's opinions of you are not your problem; they are theirs!

The best thing for you to do is be totally aware of your value. What gifts, talents, and abilities do you bring to the table like no one else? Focus on these when reaching for a particular level of success.

Success begins on the inside of you before it ever shows up on the outside. Your confidence and self-esteem mean EVERYTHING in terms of your success. If you are great at what you do but do not believe in yourself, your thoughts will overpower your work. Why do you think there are so many success stories that include people who started at the "bottom" with nothing and worked their way to the "top?" Yes, it was their work, their connections, and their opportunities, but most importantly, it was how they thought about themselves and their situation.

Never let **one** *negative situation outweigh your positive future!*

Your mind is a powerful place. Don't underestimate its power. It is the place where the money is *made* BEFORE it's ever manifested physically! This is where the creative ideas that eventually become successful inventions and endeavors are birthed. Of the tens of thousands of thoughts we produce a day, there are bound to be a few successful thoughts in there.

Stop focusing on what you don't know and don't have. As long as you are alive, you have another opportunity to acquire more; more knowledge, more wealth, and more success.

The bottom line is: Money has a spirit! It has a way of changing people. It pulls out so many emotions from people: joy, sadness, confidence, low self-esteem, generosity, greed...and the list goes on. Just be sure you are aware of what is going on as your success allows you to have more money. Be sure your intentions are always pure and your heart is right. At times, people with much wealth become corrupt. This is because with money comes power and the ability to make decisions. Now don't get me wrong. This is not ALL people. There is a great majority of people who also use their money for good and not greed. I'm simply warning you to just be careful. Be sure to be ethical in your decision-making and thoughtful in your reasoning. You are bound to make plenty of money when you do what you love and you Live ON Purpose. Just be sure to love yourself, what you do, and what you're about more than the money.

With money comes the ability to help others in a way you would not otherwise. You are able to create a platform where communities and cities can be assisted all because you combined your success and money in a way that was beneficial to many. Make quality decisions with your money and try to maintain a sense of balance. It's all about educating yourself and being true to who you are.

10

WHAT'S STOPPING YOU?

Why are you Successful?

The happiness that I bring to my family. During my journey I often keep in mind that they are my priority. Every step must be orchestrated with them in mind. Even if I misstep, I keep going. Knowing that misstep is only to correct my journey.

Betty J. K.
Account Executive

What's Stopping You?

Let's determine what is stopping you from moving forward…

FAMILY? Family has this way of deflating your brightly colored, and perfectly patterned dream really quickly. They like to use the phrase "I know you" as if that's a means to an end for your dream. Sometimes you have to back away. Stop telling them EVERYTHING. You don't even have it all clearly thought out, and they won't understand it because they are not YOU. At the end of the day, only YOU are living your life, so you cannot blame your stopping the ship on the family. In most cases, they love you and only want the best for you. Don't blame your family. It's not family. It's you…

MONEY? I get it! Even Ecclesiastes 10:19 says money answers all things, and it does. But, you cannot turn the engine completely off on your aspirations because of a lack in finances. Maybe this is a great time to get organized and very creative. Pack lunch and save money. Downsize your car and/or home. Do not live beyond your means. You can FIND the money. Be creative! It's no excuse not to move forward with your life's purpose. Sell something you no longer need!! Do whatever you must. It's not money. It's you…

TIME? "I have no time"… really? That's a lie! I must be honest. You don't want me to lie to you, do you? (Even if you wanted me to, I wouldn't!) We all have the same 24 hours a day to work with. It's how you manage those hours that makes the world of difference. Who are you holding a meaningless conversation with that stole 2 hours from your day which you will never receive back? Who did you spend time waiting for while they are running 30 minutes behind? Where did you go to spend the money you should be saving?? It's not the time. Time is money! Plan ahead how you will use your time. I'm a firm believer in having a planner. I keep a large one on my desk and a small one in my bag. The mind was not designed to remember everything. It was designed to be creative! Therefore, you must write important things down and spend less meaningless time with people and tasks. It's not time. It's you…

If you haven't figured it out…the only thing stopping you is YOU. Get out of your own way. Don't over think it but also don't settle for a lack of planning either. It's you. It's you. It's you. Now what are YOU going to do about it?? I would suggest picking up my first book, *Live ON Purpose*, to find the steps on what to do next! In it, I share 8 simple steps for you to follow in order to identify your life's purpose.

Aside from that, you need to make some clear decisions about what is no longer going to get in your way of success.

Things to reflect on and answer…

1. How much time do you spend on social media?
2. How often are you in meaningless conversations?
3. How often are you found perfecting your craft?
4. Where is your list of new ways to create revenue?
5. Who is on your list from Chapter 7 that should be removed?
6. How much productive time do you spend with family?
7. How much time do you spend meditating, thinking, or praying about your success?
8. Who is the last person with whom you shared your dream?
9. Does that person deserve to know?
10. What are the top five reasons you are not further along than you are today?
11. How organized are your days?

The answers to these questions will open your eyes to what's stopping you. It ultimately comes back to a decision. Make a decision that no matter how difficult, confusing, or trying it becomes, you will NOT stop pursuing your purpose. Someone else's purpose depends on it!

11

WHY ARE YOU A SUCCESS?

> *Why are you Successful?*
>
> *Determination and self-motivation. Motivate yourself to do what you have to do. Have passion. If you have the love for it in your heart, you'll never work another day in your life. Follow your heart. Your heart will tell you the right thing. Stop worrying about what everyone else thought about you. Three important things: Good morals, good values and be able to speak well.*
>
> **Albert S., "The Chef"**
> *Car Salesman*

Why Are You A Success?

I asked people from different age groups and multiple walks of life one question: "Why are you successful?" These are a collection of family, friends, and total strangers' responses. I love it! These responses exemplify just how different we are. Our experiences are different, but we can ALL be successful! My hope is that you find yourself somewhere in these beautiful responses. I pray they encourage you and are a constant reminder that you are indeed a SUCCESS. You are successful because you are still here. You have not given up on life. In fact, you chose to Live ON Purpose *and* Succeed ON Purpose. You are truly amazing!

Here's what they had to say:

Melvina S., Independent Business Owner
Never giving up!

Angel T., Independent Business Consultant for a Skincare Company
1. Be intentional in actions
2. Let God use you. Everything must glorify his purpose
3. Don't compare yourself to others success or fail forwards
4. Be willing to help others go beyond YOU.
5. Be willing to listen and learn. God gave you two ears and one mouth for a reason.
6. Know when what you are doing it's working and have the strength to change to see results of action.

Corrinda B., Wife
Be willing to adjust and learn from whatever you face in life.

Zulaikaha F., Educator
Never being afraid to start over...

Natasha R., Educator
My family and friends make me successful....Having people in my corner that continue to push me no matter how much I complain and make excuses. They continue to raise my bar. I've never met such stubborn and pushy people in all my life.

Rachel P.
Prayer, Patience and perspective

Donna J., Director of Nursing
Positive outlook and resiliency. Resiliency is the ability to keep
getting up and moving forward towards your goals despite adversity,
setbacks and just normal life. To do this you need to have a way to
self-inspire, have confidence in your path and gratitude in your
heart. Most of all it is about having faith that God has put you on
this earth for a divine purpose and legacy. This is your anchor and
keeps your eye on the horizon.

Erica B., Fitness Instructor
Looking over my life and what my vision of success used to be...so
much has changed. Ten years ago I would've said having a degree,
big home, large sum of money in bank account, husband, luxury car
etc. 2 years ago I decided to go for my dream of opening my own
business. I quimy FT job and answered my calling...despite being
nervous. Business has been good but it is an industry where doors
are constantly revolving. I struggled with decision to keep my space
or go back working FT. I didn't want people to say "I knew she
couldn't do it" or "Why you close...business isn't good?" When I saw
your post I knew I had to answer. NOW I see success as ME! I had
my daughter at 17, BS in Accounting at 22, married at 24 into an
abusive relationship, 2nd child at 26, MBA at 28, self-employed at
33 and divorced at 34. I don't have much money, fancy car, husband,
etc...but none of that stuff made me happy when I had it. My success
is every test God has given me and I've passed. When I have people
tell me how I've changed their lives and never stop what I'm doing.
I'm still here to tell my story. Success is my life! As my life
changes...so will my success.

Pamela C., Customer Care & Sales
Being able to sleep at night in peace, knowing that I did the best I
can do that day and didn't intentionally hurt any people nor animals.

Alicia , Acquisitions and Contract Management
In my opinion, success is heavily influenced by the people and things
in which you surround yourself. I'm a strong believer that negative

influences render negative results. Most importantly I believe in God's word; that life and death is in the power of your tongue. You have to always breathe life into your goals and aspirations. Always trust that God will never leave you and he wants to prosper you. Sometimes we can be our worse critics and supporters but you have to always think positive until the magic happens and it will if you keep pushing toward the mark. A little quote my 2nd grade teacher told us that has stuck with; "Love many, trust few, learn to paddle your own canoe."

Latoya W., Law Student & Case Manager
Starting and completing a task that we are adamant about. Success is not quitting until we get the end result of what we are trying to do.

Angela D., Nursing Student
I think that for me being successful is living a God intended life. *When I say that, I mean living life by standing on His promises that He will provide all things, with little to no fear, and living by the fruit of the spirit. In such things I believe that anything I do or venture upon will be a success. Even my failures because I dared to try.*

Joycelyn A., Independent Distributor for health and wellness products
I'm not sure I am really successful in anything yet. - Success to be is living despite the odds, now I've done that. Never giving up, despite health challenges, finances. Without God I would not be here. I could have committed suicide because of this disease but my God showed me what and who I had to live for. But He showed me that it started with me. God is my source. When everything around u changes, fails. He always stays the same. I could tell u a lot but that is the main thing that holds me together. And has despite being abused as a child and the other things that have happened. The serious car wrecks. But God said He was not finished with me yet. I know part of my gift is reaching to those that have been hurt, no matter what. I want to let them know that God loves them, and He is their everything.

Janice P., CEO President & Founder of a Consulting & Business Solutions firm

1. I'm still here at 61yrs old & I am still dreaming of the Great things to come.
2. I have had at least three different careers & excelled in them All!
3. I am still looking to learn things I have yet to know that is a measure of success in that when one ceases to strive for unknown beneficial knowledge you block further success.

Daphne Boone, Certified Nursing Assistant
Knowing my purpose and fulfilling it.

Jenny Jackson, former Career Developer
Being flexible, diplomatic and nimble.

Stephanie B., Cognitive Development Specialist
I am a success because I am a student who sits at the feet of my life. i examine patterns of thinking and feeling on a consistent basis that lead me to certain places, good and bad. I use my faults, my strengths, my successes, my missteps, my heartbreaks and most joyful moments to discover who I am and what I need to become a better version of myself. I am successful because I realize that there is no individual circumstance that defines me. I am a compilation of everything wondrous about being. I embrace it all and pray it strengthens me in purpose. I am myself....the only one that will ever be a successful me.

Tiffany H., Personal Trainer
What's makes you A Success is Putting God first in everything that you do with balance and 100%.

Jackie C., Pastor
Positively impacting people's lives with no other motive than to see them fulfill their destiny!

Why Are You A Success?

Tierra J., Crotchet business owner
I am a success because I keep God at the center of everything I do and never ever give up on my goals and dreams, big or small.

Christopher C., School Principal
Doing what you love to do without regret... Always putting others first and lastly loving God.

Travis F., Executive Assistant to a CEO
Seeing a plan come together.

Sophia H., works for a global healthcare company
Working hard and staying determine no matter what obstacles you may face.

Bonita P., Event Specialist and Owner of an Event Planning Company
Coming from a circle of very powerful entrepreneurs and marketing guru's, I was always told and firmly believe that success is not measured by how much money you have nor the amount of people in your circle. Success is measured by how many lives you impact POSITIVELY by doing what it is you do. As an event specialist, I plan events for others as well as host my own empowerment events. Nothing says "success" to me more than ensuring that I impact people's lives positively, seeing their expression of happiness at the end of their event, or receiving a simple "thank you" from one of my event attendees. Being AUTHENTIC, TRANSPARENT, & CONSISTENT at all times

Gaelen C., Nursing Student
Being a better person today than I was yesterday.

Rose S., Zumba Instructor
Learning from my mistakes! In order do better the second time around.

Gbeye N., Branch manager for a major car rental company
I've always strive to be the best in all aspects of life...that can be relationships with others, work, school, etc. Each day I'm working on being a better person than I was yesterday.

Adrianne T., United State Postal Service
Being able help others even when I'm going through something myself.

Krystal B., Hospital Office Administrator
My desire to win and unwillingness to give up until I achieve my goals!

Crystal N., CEO/Owner, wardrobe consultant, stylist & personal shopper for her own image and style agency
I would have to say my 3 strongest beliefs definitely set me up for success. They are: 1. SHUT OFF the negative self-talk or dialogue in your head. As we think, so are we - enough said. 2. There are no Big U's or Little I's - we are all the same and should be all treated with the same respect both in roles we support or in roles who support us. 3. It's Ok as long as you try...My mom always taught me to go out and TRY even if you stumble or don't succeed you can always start over. It was this support system that encouraged me to shoot for the moon, b/c even if I missed I'd be among the stars. So those 3 beliefs have been the biggest contributors to my success.

Crystal F., Entrepreneur
I know I am having success, because of many things: my faith in God, my desire to help and service others, personal development, being coachable and integrity. All of these things have attributed to my success, but I will speak to one of them. A famous motivational speaker, Jim Rohn stated, "If you help others get what they want then you will get what you want." I find this statement to be so true. When you look to achieve success you have no fulfillment, but when you are being fulfilled by what you do, your success is inevitable. Being in the health and wellness industry my fulfillment doesn't come from the money i have earned (It's just a bonus), my fulfillment comes from seeing the smile on someone's face that lost 30lbs that

had been struggling with their weight for years or someone that no longer has adult acne just from using our skincare products. I love what I do! Therefore, my success comes from helping others achieve their success!

Tara H., Owner of an art company
I am a success because I know who I am. I have figured out my purpose. A lot of people manage this but leave out one more important step. In every moment I find reason to celebrate. Even if it is a mere quantum of positive energy, I make note. Accomplish a goal? Celebrate. Dirty dishes in the sink? Celebrate. Yes... Celebrate! My family (that I love) made that mess eating food (good food) that I helped to provide. I helped someone else be successful? Bounty and celebration. I will continue to be successful because my success is not contingent upon any external source.

From Anonymous Contributors _____

What makes me successful is staying focused and watching my social circle along with my influences

Trusting that God's plan is the only way to go!

Having a family who loves and supports me. The love of God in my heart and financially living life more abundantly. These are successes individually and collectively. If I only have one of these, I feel I am just as successful as having all 3!

Knowing who I am and being confident in who I am and not ashamed of where I've been.

I am successful when I complete my goals.

I have overcome generational curses/lack. I have the vision/idea of leaving a legacy for my family/kids.

My success lies within my family. To see my children overcome hurdles and succeed. I am a success because I started school again and moved forward with change.

I am staying committed to the process of reaching short term to long term goals. Being passionate and focused on evolving into my best self that transcends to impacting people along the way.

I am successful because of hard work, dedication, and determination. Oh, and let's not forget about people, people that have been there for me from the very beginning till now!

You are successful when you:
*   Complete a task*
*   Understand a problem*
*   Resolve issues*
*   Say "I am sorry"*
*   Say "I love you"*
*   Mend a relationship*

My determination makes me successful. Giving up has never been an option. I am always trying to prove to myself that I can do better than I did the first time. I guess that makes me unstoppable.

I am successful when I trust God knowing that I am in His will. My family knowing that I love them. Always focusing on becoming a better person and helping others.

I see success through the smiles of my family members when they spend time with me because of my freedom at my 9-5.

Helping others that were once on the wrong or destructive path is success.

Why Are You A Success?

When you have arrived and are able to reach back and help others meet their dreams and goals. When you are able to see the fruit of your labor. When you are happy and content with yourself.

For me success would be fulfillment of the plan and purpose my Creator has for my life. Nothing more and nothing less.

CONCLUSION

You can and WILL do this! You already have. Give yourself the credit that is due. This time around you will spend less time putting yourself down. Begin to build up your confidence. Success looks good on you!

I hope this book has blessed your heart and mind in a way that will catapult you right into your near future. You will be amazed how well things will turn out. It does not mean you will never fail again, but now you know failure has a purpose too.

By succeeding on purpose you are giving room to others who want to do the same. You are setting an example for your family, friends, co-workers, and all the others who watch how you live.

Never forget to Live ON Purpose
and plant the seed to Succeed ON Purpose!

NOTES

ABOUT THE AUTHOR

CHRISTINA MARIE is an author, speaker, and life coach who has turned her love for teaching and helping others identify their life's purpose into a movement to help as many people Live ON Purpose as possible.

She has put these life lessons into "the little book for your big life" entitled, *Live ON Purpose* as well as her second book *Succeed ON Purpose*. These easy read guides will give you the tools you need to recognize your purpose, stop simply existing in life, know you are successful, and begin LIVING!

In addition, she continues to speak to groups about how to tap into their God-given purpose and use it to succeed in life.

When she is not writing she enjoys spending time with her husband and three children.

Never forget to *Live ON Purpose*!

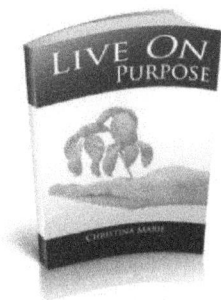

In Christina Marie's first book, *Live ON Purpose,* she explores the necessary steps to answer the age-old questions, "Why am I here?" and "What's my purpose?"

This book along with the workbook companion will give you 8 simple action steps towards finding your "what" and your "why" in life.

www.liveonpurposetoday.org

www.ingramcontent.com/pod-product-compliance
Lightning Source LLC
Chambersburg PA
CBHW051844040426
42447CB00006B/696